Journe

*Teresa of Avila's
Interior Castle*

A Reader's Guide

EUGENE McCAFFREY OCD

With a Foreword by Vincent O'Hara OCD

First published 2015 by:

TERESIAN PRESS
Carmelite Priory
Boars Hill
Oxford OX1 5HB
priory@carmelite.org.uk

ISBN 978-0-947916-18-3

A catalogue record for this book is available
from the British Library.

Quotations from the writings of St Teresa of Avila
© Washington Province of Discalced Carmelites ICS Publications
2131 Lincoln Road, N.E. Washington, DC 20002-1199 U.S.A.
www.icspublications.org

Cover images:

Statue: A sculpture of St Teresa
in front of the Monastery of the Incarnation in Avila, Spain

Butterflies: © HaveZein stock.adobe.com

Cover design by Sinéad Finn

Typeset and printed by Joshua Horgan, Oxford

Come is the love song of our race and Come
our basic word of individual wooing.
(Jessica Powers)

Contents

Foreword

The fifth centenary of the birth of St Teresa of Avila has seen the publication of myriads of new books on the saint and her message. This present publication is a notable addition to the list. It comes from the pen of a man who has already published two other books on the saint: *The Writings of St Teresa of Avila* and *Let Nothing Trouble You*. So the present volume might well be called the final one of a trilogy.

The title of the book is *Journey of Love*, and it was obviously a labour of love for Fr Eugene. He has absorbed the content of *The Interior Castle* and distilled its essence in accessible and readable language. He captures its dynamic flow and the sense of adventure that Teresa communicates – 'the great enterprise of the soul', as he expresses it so well.

The Interior Castle is the jewel in the crown of all Teresa's writings, a classic of Christian spirituality. It was written sporadically, over a matter of months, just five years before she died and at a time when her life was very fraught. There was major opposition to her reform of the Carmelite Order, and her health was deteriorating. The work is more structured than her other writings and is teeming with images – central being that of the castle. Once this image came to Teresa, it seems the words just cascaded from her pen. The beauty of the human soul opened up for her, revealing the enormous potential of every human being under the transforming love of God.

As the author points out, Teresa is writing from a standpoint of enormous spiritual experience and is looking back over the vast sweep of the journey she has come. As well as being a woman who was extraordinarily graced by God, Teresa was also a consummate teacher, and she describes the long path to union with God in lively detail, in spite of the ineffable nature of some of her experiences. She rises, at times, to soaring heights; but, ever practical, she also stays grounded in 'the bits and pieces of Everyday'. She is at her usual, cajoling best, especially when those she is addressing may be fearful of the journey ahead and are reluctant to 'launch out into the deep'.

Fr Eugene's commentary bears the hallmark of all his previous writings: simple and clear, and at times stunningly lyrical. The language is free-flowing, and the section headings are helpful and inspiring. As a work of prayer in its own right, it reads beautifully and coherently.

This book is indeed 'A Reader's Guide', for its author has an uncanny grasp of Teresa's thought, and he even manages to keep on track where sometimes she wanders off the track! His summaries of the various mansions are excellent – so good, in fact, that this little book will serve as an ideal introduction, or indeed companion, to the reader who wishes to sound the rich teachings of *The Interior Castle*.

The content of both the original and the commentary is beautifully summed up in the three terms Fr Eugene gives to the divisions of his book: *Invitation, Journey, Homecoming*. The end product is uplifting. All in all, it can be affirmed that to the jewel that is *The Interior Castle* is now added this gem of a commentary. It takes us, indeed, on a journey of love.

Vincent O'Hara, OCD
Feast of St Teresa, 15 October 2015

The Invitation

Life is a journey. And in the end, it is the journey itself that matters. It is both the starting point and the destination. Often we walk aimlessly, following a dark light, towards an unknown horizon. What if we could see a purpose, hear a call, and follow a dream – be a pilgrim rather than a wanderer, an invited guest making our way home? We *can*.

The journey is not one of many steps but one of deep longing. The treasure we seek is within, closer to us than the air we breathe, deeper than our heartbeat. We need look no further than our own secret dreams, the anxious longing and restless yearning hidden in the heart's deep core. There is a world *within*, a secret place more real and more beautiful than anything we can see *without*.

There are no preconditions. Just an invitation – a Lover's call from the centre of our own being: Come! Come, whoever you are... What if it is a different drumbeat, a road less travelled? A whisper more than a call, it is still real and alluring. Other voices contend, but the heart knows its true home. Listen! Listen to the cry of your deeper self. It was born with you and will travel with you.

Where to start? Start at the end: stand at the finishing line and look back. There is a map and a guide to show you the way. You are not alone, this is a two-way search. A light radiates from the centre to challenge the dark. Follow the light, feel its warmth, surrender to the joy of letting go. It has nothing to do with speed or strength or will power. Love is never imposed, it is offered. We are drawn, led by the leading-strings of love and, in the end, carried – like a tidal wave, towards the secret chamber of our dreams.

No one else can travel the road for you. It is your world to explore, to discover; it is for you to be part of your own creation. Of course there are obstacles, pitfalls, counter-attractions, enemies within and without – how else would you grow? How else place the seal of your love on the longing of your heart?

Enter, then. Enter within. Let not fear hold you back. The path opens up as you walk it. Only on the journey itself can the inner voice guiding the search be revealed. Let love show you the way; surrender to it, and take delight in the surprise of its unfolding.

What lies behind us and what lies before us
are tiny matters compared with what lies within us
(Emerson)

The Journey

A good way to read the Gospels is back to front. It's what is on the last page that makes sense of all the rest. That is the way it was first experienced. What transformed the disciples and turned their world upside down was not the teaching of Jesus, his miracles or his ministry, but the explosion of new life that erupted from the tomb on that first Easter Sunday morning. This was the 'Good News'. This it was that left them breathless with excitement yet stunned with amazement and confusion. Question marks became exclamation marks. Seen through the resplendent light of the resurrection, everything else made sense to them. To follow Jesus was to journey with him along the way of love, to the radiant glory of new life and new beginnings. This was the witness which they brought with them to the ends of the earth and for which they were willing to lay down their lives.

When Teresa invites us to journey with her through the myriad rooms of the castle of the soul, we must do so from the point of arrival. Otherwise, we run the risk of travelling blindly and without a purpose: not seeing the castle for the rooms; spending our time bumping into walls; falling through trap doors or lost in dark underground passages. There are 'millions' of rooms, she tells us, but only one towards which we must set our compass. It is the mission-control centre of the entire enterprise, the King's own room, a second heaven. It is from here that the light radiates and the call – the Shepherd's call – is heard.

Teresa is adamant: the rooms of the castle are not set out in order. They are everywhere – some above, some below, others to the side. Yet they dovetail, one opening onto another; what happens in one influences and supports the next. There is a unity in diversity; as in a hologram, each is part of the whole. It is almost as if each room travels with us on the journey, until we finally come to rest and find our fulfilment in the innermost abode of the castle.

> *In my end is my beginning*
> *(T S Eliot)*

Like a mountain climber who surveys the vast sweep of the landscape below, Teresa is looking back, seeing the interplay between the various 'staging posts' along the way. She is at pains to put down markers, signposts for the journey. She wants to encourage and reassure the stumbling pilgrim: don't lose sight of the bigger picture, keep your eyes set on the goal and do not be afraid. For her there is a continual two-way movement: the light and energy streaming from the centre mingle and overlap with that probing movement of the soul from the outer courts. The pilgrim soul is 'drawn' by the light, and the faint whisper of the first invitation resounds with the clarion call of the last.

The first faltering steps seem so distant and so different from the final surge towards the centre, yet they have so much in common: not least the awareness that the fullness of life flowering at the end could not have been achieved without the fragile seed planted so tentatively at the beginning. The early dwelling places of cautious commitment and joyful hope find their fulfilment in the later stages, where pain and joy intermingle in the agony and ecstasy of the surrendered heart. At the hub of the whole journey lies the fourth dwelling place, delicately holding the balance between the work of nature and the work of God. It is only when we look back over the divide and see how powerfully we have been 'carried', lifted on the breath of the Spirit, that we come to understand the meaning of the call and the richness of the gift we have received. All is gift, abundant mercy and love.

And it is this love that guides every tentative step through the castle. If we miss this, we miss not just the meaning but the joy and excitement of the journey. We will walk rather than run, fearful rather than delighting at each new adventure that opens before us. This is a love story from start to finish, from castle moat to castle keep, from the faint whisperings of hope to the exultation of the journey's end. Forget the divisions, forget the numbers, forget all the talk about 'rooms'. Think only of the call – the Lover's call – and the voice of the Bridegroom. This is your life, waiting for your simple 'yes' and the first stirrings of an enamoured heart.

> *Not knowing how close the truth is,*
> *we seek it far away*
> *(Hakuin Ekaku)*

The Interior Castle is St Teresa's masterpiece. It was the last of her major works, written five years before she died; she was sixty-two at the time. It was started, appropriately, on Trinity Sunday, 1577, in Toledo, where Teresa had been staying for nearly a year. In July she returned to Avila where she completed the book at the end of November, that same year. However, we know that for many weeks she was not able to write anything. It seems she wrote for about six weeks while she was in Toledo and then spent another five or six weeks finishing the book in Avila. Most scholars believe that the actual time spent in writing was three months, perhaps even less. An incredible feat for such a literary and spiritual classic, not unlike John of the Cross' *The Living Flame of Love* that was written in two weeks!

Not only is it astonishing that Teresa wrote *The Interior Castle* in such a short space of time, but the historical context in which she wrote makes that even more remarkable. This was the most difficult period of her life: a virtual reign of terror had been unleashed on the Carmelite reform. Her life's work was in danger of collapsing and her dream of a new, renewed, Carmel seemed on the verge of destruction. She was under house arrest in Toledo, she had been publicly condemned and censored by the Papal Nuncio, and her soul friend and companion, John of the Cross, had been kidnapped. Her health was deteriorating rapidly, and her continuing concern with the countless practicalities of the many convents she had founded was greater than ever. It is quite extraordinary that she could have found the time and energy to produce such a masterpiece, generally acknowledged as some of the finest pages she ever wrote.

Written in letters of gold
(E Allison Peers)

The Interior Castle is essentially about prayer, as indeed are all Teresa's writings. But it is about much more: it celebrates the great enterprise of the soul searching for its own deepest meaning, balanced between human longing and the divine initiative. Using the image of a castle, Teresa describes the inner journey in which the soul travels to its deepest centre, the still-point of the turning world, the place of radiant light where the fountain of living water is found, a paradise where the Lord himself finds his delight.

All Teresa's writings are, first and foremost, about God, and *The Interior Castle* is no exception. It is a book that proclaims the reality of God permeating and filling all things with his presence. Prayer is the milieu, the context in which the relationship unfolds, but the essential witness of Teresa is to that world of the spirit where God is a living God, personal, close, and totally involved in our own human existence. Teresa lived and moved in a world where everything spoke to her about God and he was part and parcel of the fabric of everyday life.

The book is 'a blending of melodies in a symphony of love',[1] a variation on a theme. It is an invitation to explore the inner world of the spirit, to grow in our relationship with God, and above all an invitation to gratitude and praise. We must never say to ourselves that it has nothing to do with those of us still struggling on the foothills of life: It is too sublime, I am out of my depth, it's something I will never experience...

Teresa writes not to disconcert us but to reassure us. She wants us to know the wonders and treasures hidden in the human heart. From knowing comes loving, and in the loving we are 'drawn' to discover for ourselves the riches and depths within the castle of the soul. There is no setting out on this journey unless we are already aware of the treasure within. Teresa admits she does not mind saying a thousand foolish things if only she could succeed in bringing us to see the deeper realities so often ignored or undiscovered. What she is describing is real, not just for her but for each of us; she is under no illusions or false imaginings. This is our call, this is our vocation, and this is the ultimate journey of every human heart.

The Interior Castle has a ring of authenticity about it. Here is a woman who *knows*. She speaks with authority, as does Jesus in the Gospels. She is not speculating. She is not quoting. She is not relying on others. She is drawing on her own experience, on the book of her own life, humbly and honestly sharing that experience with us. She is very conscious that there was a time when she herself was lost and inarticulate in the face of her overwhelming spiritual experiences. She could not understand what was happening to her and was filled with fear and self-doubt.

It was a gradual process for Teresa, first to acknowledge the *experience* – the mysterious presence of God in her life – and then, only after a long time, to *understand* what was happening to her. Finally, she was able not just to experience and understand, but to *communicate* and share her wisdom with others. She could, as Kate O'Brien so aptly remarks, enter into the presence of God with her pen in her hand and record the secrets of divine intimacy. *We* are now the beneficiaries of Teresa's gift of communication and expression.

Teresa is writing from the innermost centre of the castle. She is looking back over the vast sweep of the spiritual journey and giving a clear and brilliant outline of the road map – pointing out the supports, the dangers, the signposts, things to look for, things to avoid, things that will help and things that will diminish us. What she writes is real for her; she records it simply and clearly, without false humility or affectation. Towards the end of her life she humbly, yet honestly, admitted that she had in fact entered the 'second heaven' of the innermost castle and was experiencing the peace that goes with it – adding, with humour and diffidence, that learned men had told her she was making good progress! So much for the wisdom of the wise!

A formidable writer of prose
(Kate O'Brien)

Perhaps it would be a help at this point to say a word about Teresa's works. As a writer she is unique. She never wrote a book as such – she simply wrote *writings*. She just wanted to describe her own experience and she did so, mostly at the request of others; but once she picked up her pen, a latent talent was revealed. She had a natural gift of expressing herself in clear, simple

20

sentences, coupled with a keen intelligence, a creative imagination and a feeling for life and for people that is the stuff of all creative writing. Her human qualities of compassion, humour and basic common sense are evident on every page. She wrote from her heart and from the depth of her spirit.

As she was a natural conversationalist, her style is essentially colloquial. Indeed, she herself acknowledged that one of her difficulties was that she talked too much! Teresa wrote as she spoke; her writings, unedited and unspoiled, have lost none of their human appeal even today. This characteristic endeared her to many and was an essential ingredient in her relationship with God. In fact, her whole life – not only her prayer – was an intimate sharing among friends. She had little regard for spelling, grammar or literary style. She wrote in the local dialect, sometimes late at night, very often after a long day of travel or business. Her writings teem with countless images, allegories and personal experiences that give them a perennial freshness. Teresa could well be the patron saint of 'shop local': she refused to use anything except quality parchment, the best ink and the finest quills – all of which, she insisted, were found only in Avila! This has contributed greatly to the excellent quality of her manuscripts, still so well preserved and such a precious legacy for later generations.

Teresa was essentially a Carmelite, and all her writings must be seen in this light. The central point of Carmelite spirituality is to *be prayer in the heart of the Church* and to *help others on the journey to prayer* – to find the secret doorway within, that will open the way to the full flowering of contemplative prayer. Call it by any name you like – 'meditation', 'recollection', 'silence', 'friendship with God' – it is all an invitation towards openness and an ever-deepening movement of the spirit in the human heart. Certainly, we cannot even begin to understand the heart of this treasure within, unless we grasp its essential direction and focus.

An awesome story of the journey of the soul
(Lavinia Byrne)

When Teresa began the book in 1577 in Toledo, she was confined there by order of the Superior General and not permitted to found any more convents. Against this background her great friend, Padre Gracián, came to visit her. They spoke, among other things, about her autobiography, the *Life*, now in the hands of the Inquisition. Gracián feared that it might never be released; he also felt, perhaps, that the account was too personal for general publication. He suggested that she write another, more objective, book, incorporating her more evolved experiences from the past fifteen years. Our Lord also spoke to her, telling her not to dismiss the idea and that he would help her. The very thought of writing another book dismayed Teresa, and who can blame her! Writing in such troublesome times, with her poor health and so many business matters to attend to, she felt she would only be repeating herself like a parrot! Her one consolation was that she was writing for her own Carmelite sisters, and that women understand better than anyone the language used by women!

Teresa admits that at first she had no idea what she was going to write about. So we must jump ahead a little, to an event that happened a year or so after the book was written. She and her companions were on their way from Avila to Salamanca when they were stranded in a town called Arévalo, during a snowstorm. A good friend, Diego de Yepes, who would be one of her first biographers, also happened to be there. As they spoke long into the night, Teresa confided to him that the evening before she started writing the book, God showed her a most beautiful crystal globe, made in the shape of a castle, and containing seven mansions – in the seventh and innermost of which was the King of Glory, in the greatest splendour, illuminating and beautifying them all.

The meaning was clear and the essential structure of the book fell into place: the castle was the soul, with God at its deepest centre, and the journey inwards was an invitation to explore the myriad rooms and dwelling places of the 'interior castle'. Even Teresa could hardly have known how creative and inspirational her image was to prove, giving to the dictionary of spirituality – and to the generations after her – a new and imaginative metaphor that will always be associated with her.

> *O Pearl of great price, heaven cannot hold you,*
> *yet you choose to dwell in us*
> *(Debbie Peatman)*

The importance of beginning well can hardly be overstated, and Teresa sets the scene vividly with a variety of poetic images: a beautiful castle, a magnificent pearl, the tree of life planted beside flowing waters. From the outset, the main emphasis is on growth, beauty and endless possibilities. The greatness of the journey that now opens up before the pilgrim soul is only a reflection of the greatness of the soul itself, a whole world of wonder waiting to be explored.

It is the journey itself that matters most; the castle is not a fixed, static entity but something living, spacious and open. We ourselves are the castle, but the dwelling places within need to be discovered and explored: the castle is given, but the rooms have to be created. The dwelling places are not ready-made: we are given the tools, we are given possibilities, we are given dreams. This is the adventure, a gift of love, an invitation to be part of our own creation. It is in the soul that the mystery of God unfolds; it is here that the encounter takes place, here that the journey begins and ends.

The idea is well expressed in the Spanish word *moradas*, which literally means 'staging posts', inns along the way. We are invited to rest but not to settle; to halt temporarily but not to stop on the journey. The same idea is conveyed when Teresa speaks about the make-up of the various rooms. There is nothing small or cramped about the inner castle: there are literally rooms without number, not in order but all interconnected. We must be adventurous. The dream can only be realised once we have the courage to begin. When the journey is undertaken, the first step will eventually echo in every room in every mansion throughout the castle.

How can I be substantial if I do not cast a shadow?
I must have a dark side also if I am to be whole
(Carl Jung)

Teresa was fascinated by the beauty and grandeur of the human soul. She was unable to find anything to compare with its magnificent beauty and marvellous capacity. All the beauty comes from within, from the shining sun that is the centre of the soul, giving it such brilliance and radiance. The journey inwards is a journey towards the ever-increasing light that eventually finds its fulfilment in the splendour at the journey's end.

But Teresa is also very conscious of the darker reality, the negative side of the human experience. To be transformed by the light and power of love is the task of all spiritual endeavour, but it involves a struggle with contrary and opposing forces. From the start, she acknowledges the presence of these contrary forces, difficulties and hindrances. The darkness, however, is not caused by any flaw in the 'room' but by *the enemy within*, expressed figuratively by 'snakes and vipers and poisonous creatures'.[2] With these graphic images Teresa acknowledges the inner forces attacking and pulling against the soul.

What Carl Jung would later call the 'shadow side of our personality' and Teresa identifies as 'lizards and snakes'[3] are the harmful impulses that represent the neglected and suppressed parts of the human psyche. The battle is all too real: the emerging light struggles with the inner darkness. And it is an ongoing struggle; hence her continual insistence on the need for vigilance and for self-knowledge. Unless this shadow side of our personality is acknowledged and owned, very little spiritual progress can be made.

And behind these mischievous creatures stands a more sinister force of evil: the devil, darkness itself, the traditional figure used to indicate the source of all evil and who personifies every threat and obstacle on the spiritual journey. Teresa had too many encounters with him to be under any

26

illusions about his real work and presence. He works in hidden ways, a silent killer, 'like a noiseless file',[4] and she warns against underestimating his wiles, for he can so easily deceive us by disguising himself as an angel of light. And yet the devil, with the snakes and vipers he controls, the whole array of the 'enemy', are all part of the journey; they are fighting for their place – their destructive place – in the castle. The soul is the battleground and, in the end, must either overcome the darkness or be overcome by it.

Teresa's understanding of sin simply reinforces this truth. Sin is a denial of the light; it is the darkest blackness that obscures the sun and blocks the radiance and beauty emanating from the centre of the castle. Sin is a blocking of the light, a turning away of its brightness, a darkness needing to be challenged and ultimately transformed.

And so the scene is set, the inhabitants of the castle have been named – and the long, long journey into the light opens before the pilgrim soul. The great adventure can begin.

The real voyage of discovery consists not in seeking new landscapes, but in having new eyes
(Marcel Proust)

As we cross the threshold, Teresa seems anxious to travel as quickly as possible: the road beckons, and love's stirrings are urgent. At this point there are no detailed descriptions or clear markings, only a general feeling on the sense of direction needed. The door to the castle has come into full view, and the only way to enter it is through prayer and meditation, at least as far as Teresa is concerned; it is the way she herself has travelled.

She has great sympathy for those who have reached this point. She is at her best as a mother, supporting and encouraging. She is all too aware of the struggle between the first stirrings of an awakened love and the welter of attractions from a self-indulgent past. She is most anxious that we do not give up and fall into discouragement: even when we fall, we should not stop trying; God can write straight with all the crooked lines and broken pieces of our lives. It is a great thing to be a 'beginner': someone who has made an earnest start, who has taken those initial steps and understands the importance of not losing heart or looking back.

Light gradually begins to dawn. There is an awareness that all is not well. It is all too easy to go through the motions. But trying to respond to the call of a *different* voice is not easy, especially when we hardly know who or what it is that calls. We want to listen, to be more faithful, more open and attentive, possibly for the first time ever. Prayer filters into the heart – this is not just 'saying prayers', but something deeper than words or formulas recited by rote. The heart begins to open, the first shoots of friendship with God appear, however tenuous, and there is an awareness of a deeper hunger and thirst that up to now has hardly been noticed.

> *You called and cried out to me*
> *and broke open my deafness*
> *(St Augustine)*

This stage marks the beginning of an interest in the things of the spirit; the first stirrings of the caged heart may find comfort in prayer groups, charismatic gatherings, and faith-sharing groups. The search has begun for more solid teaching and instruction. As yet, people at this stage are hardly able to grasp the enormity of the task opening before them; only gradually can they discern the deeper vibrations of the heart and discover ways of listening and responding, however hesitantly. God speaks and works indirectly: through books and sermons, through the events and circumstances of life. He works quietly in hidden and unexpected ways, and there is an awareness of a personal providence and design at work in their lives.

Ever the realist, Teresa adds a word of caution. These people, even though they have barely started, can be idealistic, even romantic, about life and think they should become mystics and saints overnight! This is not the dwelling place where it rains manna; this is the battleground where faithfulness and determination wrestle with selfishness and idle dreams. Growth is always gradual and painful; there are no short cuts, there is no escape from sheer plod and commitment. God knows how to wait many days and even years. If the heart is right, all will be right. But there must be generosity, faithfulness and single-mindedness, come what may! The first glimmer of love, with which the search began, must now grow into something personal: friendship with Jesus, our companion along the way. This is a knowing not found in books but in the deep recesses of the pilgrim heart.

New insights emerge: humility and self-awareness cut their first teeth, and the more personal realities surface. As do a number of questions: Is there any real virtue in my life, any great depth of discipline and self-denial? When I look honestly into the mirror of my own heart, how truly charitable am I? How compassionate and sensitive to others? Am I skipping blithely along the primrose path of fantasy and self-delusion? Or maybe just going through the motions?

These and other questions begin to surface, and they are good ones for they open the door to self-knowledge and self-awareness. Often they emerge from difficulties and from a sense of failure, which may not be such a bad thing: light is always good, especially as it cuts through darkness and illusion. We discover more about ourselves from our enemies than we do from our friends; we learn more from the storm than from the calm. This is a time for planting seeds – seeds that in their own time and place will flower. Prayer is the field of sowing; here the soil will, in its own time, yield a crop of abundant fruit. Prayer is the one seed that must never be neglected; there is no option except to return to it again and again, no other means of nourishing the fragile shoots and protecting the tenuous growth.

Two roads diverged in a wood, and I –
I took the one less travelled by.
(Robert Frost)

As Teresa turns the pages and new places appear, we get the sense that she is not quite as sympathetic to the residents she now encounters! In fact, she is somewhat frustrated: a crossroads has been reached, and many hold back and go no further. It is a parting of the ways; hard decisions have to be made, which many are unable or unwilling to take. This is a place we should not be! A 'no parking' spot with double yellow lines all around! And yet, of all the dwelling places in the castle, this is the one most occupied. *Why*, when people have come so far, do they stop now?

As Teresa draws a portrait of those who have reached this point, she underlines, at the same time, the root cause of their lack of progress. They have made good strides: they live careful, well-ordered lives, they are faithful to prayer and works of charity, and will avoid sin at all costs. But they cannot bear it that the door to the further rooms is closed to them. Things are not progressing according to their plans, and patience is in short supply! This, precisely, is where the problem lies! Even the slightest contradiction or reversal to *their* plans and expectations makes them turn their backs on the journey or call a halt to it. Their lives are settled, comfortable and tidy, none of which are gospel values.

These people are exemplary in every way and for a good reason. The emphasis is on externals, on impressing others and on acceptable behaviour. So they engage in 'good works', social action and religious programmes. The real problem is that the good becomes the enemy of the better, a stumbling block to any further progress. Everything is in its proper place; reason is still very much in control; love has not yet reached the point where it overwhelms reason. They are afraid to take risks and to launch out into the deep – afraid to enter into unknown regions and leave aside their own plans and works of self-importance.

We cannot discover new oceans unless
we have the courage to lose sight of the shore
(André Gide)

Teresa herself was desperate to help but did not know how: so well-versed in virtue are these people that they think they know everything already, and it is useless to talk to them. She found in the Gospel story of the rich young man an apt example of what she was trying to describe (cf. Mt 19:16-22). From the time she began to write about this dwelling place, Teresa had this young man in mind. Here is someone who was unable to 'let go', to see beyond his own idea of 'perfection' and follow Jesus along the way of the cross. And ultimately, it is the acceptance or rejection of the cross that makes the difference. In this room of compromise, mediocrity and self-righteousness, it is the shadow of the cross that will decide. And the cross here is nothing else but the sword of truth and the pain of self-knowledge.

Humility and self-awareness are almost synonymous for Teresa; we are not aware of the deep roots of sinfulness in each of us, or the need to put the axe to the root of the tree. 'Test us, Lord –,' Teresa cries, 'for You know the truth – so that we may know ourselves.'[5] And, of course, he will, for his love is ever-active and creative; he will use every means to draw us to himself. He will disturb our comfortable world with the shadow of the cross: failure, disappointment, misunderstanding and opposition, dismantling the protective scaffolding of our small, self-contained world. He will seek ways of breaking down the barriers of control and complacency. The scene is once more set for a new and far greater leap of faith and surrender than could ever have been imagined.

A *terrible beauty is born*
(W B Yeats)

Teresa is now very conscious that we are entering into a whole new world: one of contemplative prayer and mystical grace. When she writes of this in the *Life*, she speaks about another life, a new one, different from what she has already experienced: a life that is not her own, but one that God has begun to live in her.

This is the place of transition; the whole spiritual landscape has changed. We are at a bridge, a new crossroads; a chasm has opened up, one that we cannot cross by ourselves. We are no longer in control: we have to be led, carried like a child in its mother's arms. The landscape is different, the way of 'travelling' is different, and the inner spring has found a new and purer source. Everything has changed utterly, 'a terrible beauty' is born,[6] a beauty that becomes even more terrifying as the inner journey progresses. Teresa calls it 'supernatural', but the word has a different connotation for us today. She is really speaking about the beginning of contemplative prayer.

Contemplation has nothing to do with who

we are or what we are, with being set apart or having a special calling. Contemplatives are found everywhere; there are as many contemplatives in the kitchen as in the cloister, in the workplace as much as in a monastery. It is a way of life, a way of seeing, and a way of 'being' in relation to God, a place where silence and stillness speak volumes. Essentially, it is about God's initiative, not ours: a 'gift' freely given and totally unmerited. The essence of contemplative prayer is surrender, openness and a willingness to let go. Here, God acts directly on the human heart, transforming it into his own image and likeness.

This is the time of decision, of letting go in a great leap of faith; a surrender much easier to talk about than to achieve! Here, for the first time, God becomes real for us, and his love becomes individual and personal – the soul now 'knows' that God is within. Not in the sense of head knowledge, of ideas or concepts, but knowledge that is personal and experiential. Up to this time, our efforts have been slow and laborious. Now the deeper vibrations and movements of the spirit begin to work. It is a movement away from our own efforts and towards accepting God's initiative; a movement towards transcendence and away from self-interest.

In our tidy, well-ordered life, cracks begin to appear. We do not have the answers; we do not even ask the right questions any more. In fact, we stop asking questions and we begin to listen. We become aware of the deep flaws and wounds in our character: the broken cisterns that hold no water. The shadow within casts a long, dark line, and we stumble, limping through the dim rooms of the castle. There is a death and a birth and we are being asked to enter by the narrow gate. Psychologically and emotionally, something is dying; spiritually, something new is being born. The body laments for what it has lost, but the spirit rejoices at what it has found.

Your road may lead through darkness
but it will lead to you
(Anon)

A new and different understanding of God begins to emerge. The veil between heaven and earth grows thin. God is no longer 'out there' but 'within', no longer an 'idea' or an 'image'. He is bigger than any thoughts we may have of him, he is outside categories and boundaries. As our understanding changes, so too does our way of praying. Prayer becomes an awareness of presence, an intimate sharing in the silence of waiting. A change in the movement of my life takes place: from thinking to loving, from ideas to attentiveness, from doing to being, from planning and organising to trust and surrender. Here is a new and impossible God; our relationship with him is no longer ours to control or contain.

At first, the movement is almost imperceptible. There is no way to pinpoint this action of God working more directly in our soul: it is as unexpected and unpredictable as the first experience of falling in love. Like a boat crossing a lake when of a sudden a wind fills the sail, the direction is unchanged but the boat is carried along by the added movement of the breeze. Someone else is guiding: the breath of the Spirit begins to support our feeble efforts. God does more and more, and we do less and less. He must increase, I must decrease.

Teresa forages for her own image and almost inevitably returns to her favourite theme of water. In the *Life*, prayer is the water that irrigates the garden of the soul, and in *The Way of Perfection* it is a symbol of the living water that Jesus promised the Samaritan woman. In *The Interior Castle*, Teresa skilfully uses the image of filling a basin with water. This can be done either with *pipes and aqueducts* that fill the basin gradually and slowly with much noise and a lot of hard work, or by a *spring* that flows directly into the basin and fills it quietly and more effectively. The spring is the image of the inflowing action of God's grace, working quietly in the human heart.

Teresa uses two Spanish words to capture further this change of direction: *contentos*, which means a sense of satisfaction or contentment; and *gustos*, which is probably best translated as a feeling of spiritual joy and delight. Satisfaction in this sense is something we can experience in very many human activities, including prayer; spiritual delight is something that comes from God. The basic difference is in the *source* of the experience: one is mediated through our own efforts; the other is gifted through the immediate action of God – it cannot be manipulated or manufactured. One has its source in human nature and ends in God; the other has its source in God and ends in human nature. Teresa compares the awareness of this loving presence to a scented perfume placed on burning coals, filling the whole house with its fragrance.

One does not surrender a life in an instant.
That which is lifelong can only be surrendered
in a lifetime
(Elisabeth Elliot)

How we react to such a significant spiritual and psychological shift is vital. We have to accept that we are no longer in control and that the power of the Spirit is working actively in our lives. We cannot manipulate God or control his action; we are in the world of pure gift and boundless, unmerited grace. Our part is to surrender, to persevere and to let go: to open the heart to God's free gift of himself. Teresa is trying to draw a map, an outline, but she would be the first to acknowledge that the map is not the territory. The journey for each one is personal, with its own form and contours. Yet there is a great sense of reassurance in knowing that something special and beautiful is taking place. Despite all the disorientation and confusion, there is an intimation that the way we are being led points beyond the limits of our horizon.

It is also important to remember that every gift, every touch of God, affects us in different ways. There is the *experience itself*, and then there is the *more permanent, positive effect* that comes with it. The experience can be one of either joy or pain. There can be a sense of wholeness and a deepening of love and humility. But it can also be one of pain, loss and confusion. More and more, the un-spiritual self emerges and we become aware of our wounds, our failures and our vulnerability: the dark shadows of the un-graced self appear. Yet, unless we embrace the shadows, we cannot embrace the truth. Unless we accept our own 'sacred wounds' and our own brokenness, we cannot grow into wholeness – it is through the chinks and cracks and the broken pieces of our life that God enters.

We ourselves may feel a sense of shame, failure and defeat, crying out like Peter: 'Depart from me, Lord, for I am sinful' (Lk 5:8). There can be a real sense of agony and despair, but underneath it all God is working. And it is this hidden, permanent grace that matters most: the deeper transformation of the heart. *This is always there.*

When God enters a human soul and touches the heart, it is for one purpose only: to awaken love, a love seeking only to give and to receive. In the end, nothing else matters; nothing else is real but God's love for us and our love for him – the first and the greatest commandment.

The house of my soul is too narrow for you to come in; let it be enlarged by you (St Augustine)

At this point, Teresa quotes one of the Psalms to illustrate what she is speaking of: 'the enlarging of the heart' (cf. Ps 119:32). In order to make space for the inflowing of mystical grace it is essential for the heart to be expanded. Contemplation enlarges the heart, stretching its capacity to love. It is the beginning of the process of growth – towards the divine and the letting go of the narrow confines of self. It also draws the soul into greater silence and stillness.

The prayer that characterises the fourth dwelling place is what Teresa calls the *prayer of quiet*. The 'quiet' in question is a quietness of the will: the soul is held by God, like a child carried at the breast. The intellect and the imagination do not share in this stillness, so the mind is plagued by a thousand thoughts and distractions. In fact, the mind is incapable of understanding what is taking place and there is very little the soul can do except try not to struggle, accept the situation, and make acts of love. Here Teresa gives her famous principle that cuts to the very heart of contemplative prayer: 'the important thing is not to think much but to love much; and so do that which best stirs you to love.'[7]

There is a dual process taking place: attachment and detachment, attachment to God and the things of God and a deeper detachment from all that hinders or blocks his embrace. God is gradually drawing the soul away from created things and at the same time drawing it to himself. At one and the same time, contemplation both cleanses and purifies; it divides and unites. The heart knows only too well the things that hold it in a selfish bind, but it needs the greater and stronger inflow of grace to loosen the ties.

The only journey is the one within
(Rilke)

As we journey with Teresa towards the deeper, inner regions of the castle, we realise how very conscious she is of the task set before her and of the difficulties she now encounters. She even poses a question for herself, wondering in fact whether it would be better not to say anything about these things; after all, it is almost impossible to speak of them because, for the most part, the mind is not capable of understanding them. Even comparisons are of little avail, for they are quite inadequate to express what is happening at this stage of the journey.

Yet Teresa begins the opening page of the fifth dwelling place with the consoling and quite remarkable affirmation that there are very few who do *not* enter this dwelling place! And she is not speaking of her Carmelite sisters alone. She admits that there are many 'ways' of being present – presence is much more than simply being there. Some will do no more than reach the door, never passing beyond the entrance; others will venture still further, drawn by the wondrous light radiating from the centre. But for Teresa, even to come within the threshold of this dwelling place is in itself something very special and beautiful.

One of the things Teresa hoped for, at the beginning of the book, was that even those who may never experience the further reaches of the innermost rooms will come to know the riches and treasures hidden in the human heart and praise the ever-loving wonders of grace. After all, it is not necessary to experience the presence of God at every level and in every dimension. God gives his gifts in different ways to different people. What is important is that we should be open and ready for what he has in mind for us. Teresa is adamant: this journey has nothing to do with bodily strength, intelligence or will power. It is a *journey of the heart*. It is a work of love and of surrender; it is about conformity of my will to the will of God: a death to self and a rising to new life.

> *My heart sits on the arm of God.*
> *Like a tethered falcon. Suddenly unhooded.*
> *(Hafiz)*

Teresa often speaks about what she calls the *prayer of quiet*. It was a familiar term in her day, but does not rest as easily on modern ears. As seen, the 'quiet' in question is in the will – the will as the faculty, or power, of *loving*. So the heart is held in quietness and stillness, focused on God, even though the thoughts and the imagination are quite distracted and restless. God 'touches' the soul in such a way that it cannot doubt his presence and closeness.

We may feel the same uneasiness when Teresa speaks about the *prayer of union*; it is easy to be daunted by the expression. Essentially it is a prayer of deeper, more personal, intimacy with God. It is an experience not just of closeness or nearness, but of oneness and togetherness. It is union, it is unity. Once the threshold of the fifth dwelling place has been crossed, the rest is an ever-deepening journey into the transforming grace of contemplative prayer. The soul is coming to know God as love, a love poured into our heart by the Holy Spirit. This is like the experience of 'falling in love', of being drawn into an embrace of divine intimacy. There is also a feeling of 'being loved' unconditionally: the soul is in God and God is in the soul.

But the fact remains that it is difficult to express in words the experience now taking place. In a more scriptural way, we are speaking about the fullness of Christian love flowering within: the Gospel coming to full fruition in the human heart. The soul is being shaped and formed into the image and likeness of Christ, becoming another Christ. Love is at work, friendship is flowering, and the soul is transformed into an unshakable love: love of God and love of neighbour.

The flame of the Everlasting Love
Doth burn ere it transform
(Cardinal Newman)

We must not think of such experiences as a state of continual peace and happiness! Far from it! There are indeed 'touches' of divine intimacy, times when the soul is deeply aware of God's love and presence. But there are other times – and they are far more frequent – when the experience of God is one of absence, loss and even dereliction. The experience itself is generally short and fleeting; it can be one of joy or pain, light or darkness, presence or absence. What matters is the impact, the lasting effect, something over which we have no control, like a burning brand that leaves an indelible imprint on the soul.

Teresa admits she does not understand how God makes himself present within the soul; she compares this to his sudden emergence from the sealed tomb or his unexpected appearance in the Upper Room. But she had no doubt as to why he comes and what is the effect of his presence. He comes to enrich the soul by his gifts and to awaken within it a living faith, a resolute hope and an unselfish love. Here, her teaching, her experience, overlaps with that of John of the Cross: the only sure and safe road along the spiritual journey is the way of dark faith, poverty of spirit and a 'living flame of love' that must 'burn ere it transform'.

The lover's heart is gradually drawn away from all that hinders growth and diminishes life, to a letting go of spiritual illusion, pretence and self-deception. At the same time, there is a deepening of all that nourishes and fosters love. We are moving into a different world where we begin to see the hundreds of lies and deceptions presented as reality. New values and new horizons open up; the pretence and the games that are played everywhere fade into insignificance, like children laying aside their toys and turning towards more substantial realities.

It is no wonder, Teresa says, that the poor soul is often confused and dejected, suffers from anxiety and is afraid that it is on the wrong road. She is speaking from painful experience. She suffered tremendously at this stage of her life because of the lack of wise and prudent guidance. There were very few who understood her or believed her experience to be genuine. She thought, for a long time, that she was being deceived either by the devil or by her own imagination. She was often badly advised, by 'half-witted' theologians who did not understand the ways of God or the workings of the Holy Spirit, and who only added to her pain and confusion. No wonder she so often emphasises self-knowledge, humility and common sense.

> *You were born with wings.*
> *Why prefer to crawl through life?*
> *(Rumi)*

Teresa turns once again to images and metaphors to help her express what she is trying to say, even though she had said earlier that all comparisons were inadequate. She seems to have found exactly what she wanted in the metaphor of the *silkworm* and the *butterfly*, one of the most famous and certainly one of the loveliest of all her images.

Teresa was fascinated by the idea of the silkworm, although she admits she never actually saw one! She describes it skilfully, using it to illustrate the transformation now taking place. The silkworm begins as a tiny egg, a larva that feeds off the mulberry leaf, and from it a little caterpillar gradually emerges. The caterpillar attaches itself to a twig and begins to spin strands of silk to enfold itself within its own cocoon. Inside the cocoon the caterpillar seems to 'die', but is gradually transformed into a lovely butterfly. It has undergone a *complete transformation*: the silkworm, which is large and ugly, comes out of the cocoon a beautiful white butterfly. For Teresa, the cocoon represents an ever-deepening relationship with Christ in which the soul is immersed. Nourished by the light and heat of the Spirit, the soul is changed – transformed – into something it could never have imagined: a beautiful, free, yet delicate butterfly.

Teresa needed this image. The castle was not creative enough for her. It did not express the sense of freedom and growth of which she wanted to speak. The image of the butterfly captures the transformation now taking place: not just of growth but of a new way of being, a metamorphosis, a transformation of something quite ordinary, like a worm or a caterpillar, into something quite extraordinary and exquisite, a beautiful butterfly.

Teresa's emphasis, though, is not so much on beauty as on *freedom*. The soul has been liberated, it has broken its bonds and is no longer earth-bound. Why crawl when you can fly? Why stay within the limits of a mulberry leaf when the vast horizons of the open sky can be explored? Yet, for all its new-found freedom, the little 'butterfly' is 'restless'! It has not yet attained the full possession of the Beloved. It wants to fly away and be with its God, and it cannot rest anywhere that does not give it that fruition. It is torn between the joy of freedom and the pain of unrequited love. Restless, yearning, searching, longing – these are the words Teresa uses, and they open up for her the avenue into the sixth dwelling place.

A place where lovers meet
(Susan Muto)

Teresa now sets aside the symbol of the butterfly and turns to another comparison to develop her thought further. This she finds in the metaphor of *marriage*, which symbolises the love-relationship between God and the soul. In fact, it is the image of marriage that holds together the last three sections of the book and gives them their unity. She realises it is only a rough comparison but cannot find another that would explain better what she is trying to say. She outlines the different 'stages' of marriage: the *meeting* of the two lovers, the *engagement*, and the *marriage* itself. Each of these represents for her the growth and development of the last three dwelling places: the meetings, the intimate 'encounters' between God and the soul; the engagement; and the final 'union of love' that finds its completion in the innermost room of the castle.

48

There are, first of all, the preliminaries: God and the soul are getting to know each other. All the lovely things that happen in the full flush of first love are taking place: the attentiveness of love, the exchange of gifts, the longing to be together, and the sharing of time and presence. God is gradually overshadowing the soul, letting it know the depths of his love, and drawing the soul to an even more complete and total surrender.

The symbol of marital love automatically suggested to Teresa another scriptural image, taken from the Song of Songs, one of the most beautiful and luxuriant love poems ever written. In spite of having only one reference to God, it has always been interpreted as an allegory of the love-relationship between God and Israel – or, for Christians, as a symbol of the love of Christ for his Church and for each individual. It has inspired the writings of many of the saints and mystics. Basically, it is a series of passionate love poems in which the lover and the beloved – the bride and the bridegroom – ardently seek for, and ultimately find, each other in an embrace of love.

Teresa refers to only two verses from the Song of Songs: the image of the *wine cellar* and that of the *bride*, distracted and distraught, searching everywhere for her beloved. The wine cellar is the place where lovers meet and where the most intimate exchanges take place. The bride is 'brought' there: she does not go by herself, she is 'drawn' by the beloved; she finds him who has found her. The wine, a symbol of joy and inebriation, often overflows and finds expression in the foolishness of love; at one and the same moment, it can be all praise, all joy, and carried away by excess. It is not right to judge by rational standards. Teresa would echo St Paul's phrase, 'we are fools for Christ' (1Cor 4:10), for love does foolish things. Who wants a love that is reasonable, controlled, calculating, and never puts a foot wrong? If love does not dream dreams and strive for impossible things, it hardly deserves the name. Love has its reasons which reason does not understand.

In His will is our peace
(Dante)

The whole purpose of contemplative prayer is to bring about a loving union of our will with the will of God. That is what the spiritual journey is all about. The way Teresa was led is not for everyone. God does not give everyone a direct 'experience' of his presence or special favours. There is another way: the way of faithfulness, the way of generosity, the way of surrender; the way of trying to do the will of God in our everyday life. That is the purpose of every stage of the journey: to say and to mean 'Your will be done.'

Dante's lovely phrase comes to mind, 'In His will is our peace.' Sadly, we often react negatively to the idea of God's will: we think it is something imposed on us, something that constrains our freedom, something that we have to 'accept'. We forget that *God's will is no different from his love and is an expression of it.* The one thing God wants is our good; he wants to love us and awaken our hearts so that we can 'live through love in his presence' (Eph 1:4). The way of special favours is not for everyone, nor is it essential, but the way of love *is.* Love is a decision – a decision to open our hearts to the gift of God's love and to follow the way of the Gospels to the best of our ability. God does not impose his will: he invites us and draws us to himself with 'leading-strings of love' (Hos 11:4).

For our part, the essential response is one of 'trying'. We can achieve the fullness of Christian love if we try to respond to this invitation as best we can, and open ourselves to the gift of this love. If you love me, you will keep my commandments, Jesus reminds us; and they are, in the end, summed up in the simplest way: to love God and to love one another. All too often we try to impose our will on God, make demands and expectations of him, play games and put God to the test. But the real and decisive test is the way we *live* our lives, and the quality of our love.

The way of the surrendered heart
(Carolyn Humphreys)

The sixth dwelling place covers eleven chapters; it is by far the largest section in the whole book.

Of all her writings, it is the most personal and autobiographical. It is Teresa's own story of the graces, favours and mystical experiences so bountifully bestowed on her, and of the many difficulties and trials that accompanied them. These pages celebrate the grace of engagement and the whole experience of purification and transformation that go with it: the way of the surrendered heart drawn ineffably into an experience of divine love.

It is a journey of surrender – a long, frightening, painful surrender. Long psychologically, long emotionally, long spiritually, long chronologically – because, Teresa says, people have to spend many, many years before they are brought into the innermost region of the castle. For Teresa, it was important to record her experience. There was very little written about it in her day, and she wanted to pass on the knowledge and wisdom she had acquired to her Carmelite sisters and to those who could benefit from it.

In this dwelling place, God's action is much more intense than anything that went before: an intimate communication of divine love is poured into the human heart. It is a journey in which the soul experiences, in a very personal and existential way, the 'immeasurable riches of Christ' (Eph 2:7). This is not just a phrase quoted from St Paul, this is a *reality*. Here, deep knowledge and joy go hand in hand with deep suffering and pain as the soul is torn between the experience of the crucified Christ and that of the risen Lord of glory. Returning to the image already used of 'the expansion of the heart', here the heart is being stretched to its full capacity to receive the inflowing of grace. God is working with great power in a deep, personal way in the soul, drawing it into complete and total surrender.

> O *living flame of love*
> *that tenderly wounds my soul*
> *in its deepest centre*
> *(John of the Cross)*

Teresa, like John of the Cross, speaks of a 'wound of love',[8] a phrase that now finds its full meaning and fulfilment. God has become 'the Hound of Heaven',[9] wooing the soul like a jealous lover asking for that which 'costs not less than everything'.[10] He wants everything, and he will take everything because he wants to *give* everything. Nothing, absolutely nothing, must be held back. There must be a total self-surrender – a surrender that the soul cannot make of itself, no matter how much it wants to. For Teresa, this surrender was accomplished by the many special favours and graces she received, but essentially it takes place through the profound working and power of the Holy Spirit. Nowhere are these words of Scripture more appropriate: 'God is a consuming fire' (Hb 12:29).

The distinguishing factor compared with anything that went before is one of degree: everything is magnified. The state of interior prayer is deepened; the depth of the spiritual life is intensified, as is the degree of pain and suffering that is experienced. Here, we have the nearest parallel to the writings of John of the Cross, especially in *The Dark Night of the Soul*. Both Teresa and John describe meticulously the level and the depth of purification that is needed before God can unite the soul to himself in love. Teresa, for the most part, locates this suffering in external causes, perhaps as a reflection of her own life, so involved was she with the daily burdens of administration, and plagued by jealousy, opposition and misunderstanding. John of the Cross, on the other hand, focuses more on the direct action of God and the work of the Holy Spirit. But the essential point for both of them is that this is the work of God. This is not happening by chance: it is the work of the Spirit, preparing, cleansing and purifying the soul.

The symbol of love is not the heart, but the cross
(Anon)

The sixth dwelling place is essentially a sharing is the mystery of the cross, the cross in all its frightening darkness and dereliction – the fear and agony in the garden, the rejection and the abandonment of Calvary: My God, my God, why, *oh why*, have you forsaken me? Everything is falling apart. The little ways in which the soul until now has protected itself – the evasions, the hiding places – are no more. Now there is only the desert, and in the desert there is nowhere to hide.

We cannot find our way out of the desert unless someone leads us. There are no signposts; there is nothing but sand and more sand and we do not know north from south, east from west. The supports that have sustained us are taken away, and the structure that has been built up and cautiously held on to is being dismantled. The light, the assurance that once gave strength and sustenance, is no more. There is a real sense of being lost, a sense of going nowhere. The little butterfly, that seemed so free and so close to everything it longed for, now seems to have lost everything. There is gnawing self-doubt, remorseless agonising, and the perennial fear of deception and delusion.

In the end, *there is nothing left but love* – nothing else to sustain the soul, even though it is convinced that, in fact, it does not love. This is the *nada* of John of the Cross in its most terrible aspect: nothingness for the sake of everything, lovelessness for the sake of love, death for the sake of life. The only thing that remains is love: a profound love that ultimately becomes indestructible and is the only thing that will carry the soul on the rest of this journey.

'Wounding' is an accurate expression as the soul is torn between ardent yearnings and restless desires. The soul has a sense of being drawn away from its own centre and yet not knowing where it is going; searching, like the bride in *The Spiritual Canticle*, for her Beloved, or like Mary Magdalene weeping at the tomb for the One she has lost. When the soul is aware that God is near and present, there is joy and jubilation; when he seems absent, there is nothing but pain and desolation. God is invading the soul, possessing it in a certain sense, taking what the soul wants to give but cannot, moulding and reshaping it to receive the ultimate gift of himself.

> *The only wisdom we can hope to acquire*
> *Is the wisdom of humility: humility is endless*
> *(T S Eliot)*

In the sixth dwelling place, Teresa records some of the extraordinary spiritual favours and graces she has received: visions, ecstasies, and words of love spoken to her by Christ. While profoundly humbled by these experiences, she was at the same time filled with an ineffable peace and a love that sought only to surrender and give itself in unselfish service. Her Beloved found countless ways to encourage her and support her in her undertakings, and to reveal to her the grandeurs and mysteries of his will.

In this context she tells of a profound insight

she received in relation to humility, a subject never far from her thoughts. Once she was wondering why humility was such an essential disposition when it suddenly struck her that God is supreme Truth, and that 'to be humble is to walk in truth'.[11] Of ourselves we are nothing, everything we have and everything we are comes from him; and if we do not acknowledge this we are walking in falsehood: *We have to be nothing – nothing so that God can make us something.* She is not speaking of the truth in the sense of not telling lies, but rather of a truth that is the fulfilment of all truth: that God alone is absolute truth and everything else, compared with him, is nothingness and emptiness. To enter the final dwelling places, the soul must be free of all illusions and lies; it must be totally rooted in the truth of its absolute dependence on God; and, in the end, come to know that everything is sheer 'gift' and abundant mercy.

In all this, it is important to remember that Teresa is describing her own personal journey. For her, these experiences were very palpable, sometimes overwhelmingly so, and at times all too public. But for other people, the vast majority, this is not necessarily so. One has only to think of Thérèse of Lisieux, who never experienced any such mystical favours, yet her desires and longings were for her 'a real martyrdom'.[12] God was working so deeply and secretly in her that even those closest to her were not aware of the 'infinite horizons' that love's urgent longings inspired in her.

*Let me hear your voice: for your voice is sweet
(Song of Songs)*

One of the central themes in all Teresa's writings is the role of Christ in the spiritual journey and especially along the path of prayer. She writes passionately about it and is ready to argue her point with anyone, even with those learned men who seem to disagree with her. As always, she can confirm everything she says by the fruit of her own experience. She had already spoken about this in her *Life*, where she laments the mistake she once made of thinking that somehow devotion to Christ was an impediment to contemplative prayer. Fifteen years later, she now feels the need to return to the subject again – to reinforce her own experience of Christ and the central reality of his presence in her life.

She especially wants to warn against the danger of false mysticism and any sort of unhealthy disregard for the human reality. Essentially that would be a denial, not only of our humanity but also of the beauty and mystery of the Incarnation. We are not angels, we are of the earth, with bodily needs that must always be acknowledged and respected. It is a false and pernicious trap to separate the spiritual from the secular. Christ, his mother Mary and the saints did not live in a vacuum. God comes to meet us as we are and where we are and is always to be found in 'the bits and pieces of Everyday'.[13] Christ is the way; for Teresa there is no other. Whether we travel along the foothills or the valleys or on the higher mountain paths, he is our companion, our guide and our fellow traveller.

But there is another, very practical, question for Teresa: Where is Christ in the experience of contemplative prayer? After all, we are told that contemplative prayer is an imageless prayer, a 'dark knowledge' of God[14] flowing unimpeded into the soul. The answer is not in turning away from Christ, but in understanding the various ways in which he comes to us and the ways in which we respond. One is the way of thoughts, images, words and reflections: a conversation with Christ that moves from reflection to a loving dialogue. This is a good way, and one we must come back to again and again. But there is another way. Many people cannot meditate in such an orderly or structured manner, not just because their minds are too restless and distracted but because they are being led along a new and different path. 'Meditation', as they know it, is not just burdensome but impossible; they have come to the end of one way of prayer and are being drawn into another, the way of contemplative prayer.

The soul now needs a simpler and more intuitive way of praying; there is no need to conjure up images and thoughts of Christ or of divine things. Often a word, a phrase or single sentence will be sufficient to bring the mind into stillness and silence. The mind and heart are 'open' to perceive the deeper reality and rest quietly in it. There is no need to focus on precise details or images: the heart is held in awareness, aware that he is present, that he is near, and that he loves us.

This is the beginning of contemplative prayer, the movement away from words and thoughts to something more interior and silent: less talking and more listening, the mind hushed in quietness. What matters is that we enter into this presence and that we are not afraid to 'rest' in it. Christ is not bypassed or ignored; rather, there is an invitation to enter more deeply into the mystery of his love, and to become still more closely united with him.

> *Love is an endless mystery,*
> *for it has nothing else to explain it*
> *(Tagore)*

How do we even begin to speak about the innermost region of the castle? Human language is limited, ciphers on a page; symbols and images fall apart. Teresa herself feels this inadequacy and wonders if it would be better to say nothing and just finish with a few words. There is even a sense of anticlimax about it all. The high drama and turbulence of the previous stages give way to quietness and a sense of rest and completion. The light radiating from the innermost chamber flows gently and wordlessly into the soul. The little butterfly has at last found rest close to the heart of the Beloved. The seventh dwelling place is God's own dwelling place. For just as he dwells in heaven, so he has a special place deep within each person where he alone dwells. This is the innermost and deepest centre of the soul, the second heaven, the abode of peace.

A new and startling world is now revealed to the soul, something 'no eye has seen, no ear has heard' (1Cor 2:9), welling up from the glowing centre of love at the heart of the castle. No longer is it very difficult to describe, it is impossible to do so. What is revealed is not just the presence of Christ or an ever-deepening relationship with him, but an encounter with the living God, revealed in the very heart of the Trinity. Through a wondrous knowledge, too exquisite to describe, the most profound truth of all is *unveiled*, and the scales are removed from the eyes of the soul. The culmination of the mystical journey is an entrance into the mystery of the Triune God: Oneness hidden in the heart of the Three.

What Teresa once accepted by faith she now understands by inner sight. All three Persons communicate themselves to her, speak to her and explain those words of our Lord in the Gospel:

that he and the Father and the Holy Spirit will come and dwell with the soul that loves him and keeps his commandments (cf. Jn 14:23). It was as if she was almost able to 'see' the three persons of the Trinity engraved on her soul and was unable to think of any one of them without realising that all three are there. Now there is direct, immediate knowledge and perception, not just of Christ but of the Trinity.

Not only is there a new understanding of the mystery of God, there is also an explosion of new life, a sharing in his creative, redemptive energy. It may be an 'abode of peace' but not one of 'rest' or inactivity. This is a peace with a difference: a substantial peace, hidden in the inner depths of the soul, 'a peace the world cannot give' (Jn 14:27). It is not something on the surface, a state of bliss or unruffled calm. If anything, it is a launching pad for an eruption of new initiatives and fresh adventures.

Life rolls on in unrelenting challenges amid a maze of personal problems and everyday decisions. Teresa received the grace of spiritual marriage ten years before she died. Her work as foundress was far from finished, and she had yet to face the stinging opposition launched against her reform from ecclesiastical powers, municipal authorities and betrayal by many of those closest to her. Although her health was in decline, she still had many miles to travel, two major books and hundreds of letters to write; she was a pilgrim in the service of her Beloved, a fool for Christ.

The spiritual energy and apostolic zeal that now flooded her life could be fulfilled only in selfless service and in a passionate zeal for the Church and for the coming of the kingdom. This is what drove her from one length of Spain to the other: to establish, each time, an oasis of prayer and intercession for the Church where Christ would be King, his mother would be honoured, and the Blessed Sacrament would be reserved. In this stage, the soul is endowed with the life of God, radiating from its deepest centre and transforming its every action. It both rests in the divine presence and shares in his creative action in the world. Very simply, everything is now different – a new reality and a whole new world.

One word frees us of all the weight and pain of life:
that word is love
(Sophocles)

It is easy to be daunted by some of the words used in the later stages of the spiritual journey. They give the impression of something extraordinary and esoteric, out of the reach of the average pilgrim. Perhaps so, but it is the reality that matters, not the words. *The Interior Castle* is essentially the story of a love – a love in which all other loves are ultimately consumed; each new step opens up a different face of the multifaceted diamond. The journey is towards the abode of love, the radiant light emanating from the innermost chamber.

Love is the same, whether human or divine: it does foolish things, it breaks its own rules. God is the tremendous Lover, and all his saints share the same 'madness'! It is best not to speak in rational terms, but in the language of the cross, the language of the Last Supper, as Jesus invited his disciples to share his mission, abide in his love and enter into the intimate unity of the Father, Son and Spirit. This is the fullness of the life of the spirit, the experience of perfect charity and the full flowering of Christian love. The soul has 'put on Christ' (Gal 3:27), is transformed into his image and likeness, and through him enters into the mystery of all mysteries, the intimate life of God.

This is the love that brought Love down from heaven, the love that ushered in the kingdom of God and was revealed in the intimacy of the Upper Room. This is the love that lay prostrate in the garden, experienced abandonment on the cross and yet rose in the glory and power of Easter morning. The love that Teresa is speaking about is the charity that burned in the heart of Christ from Bethlehem to Calvary, from the wilderness of Judea to the garden of the resurrection. It is an active, dynamic love that poured itself out for the salvation of the world. Now, at the still-point of her burning world, she becomes another Christ

– consumed with the same passion and mission for the glory of the Father and the spread of the kingdom.

But Teresa cannot leave the subject without searching for images, even though they can only ever be an awkward reflection of the truth. She speaks of *two lighted candles* coming together to form one light, one flame. But this is inadequate, as they can be separated again and so do not express the depth of the union that has taken place. She turns again to her favourite image of *water*: raindrops falling on the river or a stream – all is water, for the rain that falls from heaven cannot be divided or separated from the water of the river. The image of *light* also suggests itself to her: a room into which a bright light enters through two windows – although divided when it enters, the light becomes one and the same. Finally, she returns to her previous image of the *wine cellar* from the Song of Songs: here, the soul drinks deeply of the wine flowing abundantly from the heart of the Beloved, a wine that enriches all her activities, making her a servant of love.

In the end, all these are only images, faltering images. Something Teresa herself acknowledges: 'These comparisons make me smile and I do not like them at all, but I know no others. Think what you will; what I have said is the truth.'[15] All shadows merely of this incredible truth: that God and the soul are *one* – in a union that is ineffable

and indissoluble, beyond symbols, beyond comparisons, beyond words.

> *Love does not consist in gazing at each other,*
> *but in looking outward together*
> *in the same direction*
> *(Antoine de Saint-Exupéry)*

Not surprisingly, Teresa ends the final pages of
The Interior Castle with the story of Martha and
her sister Mary. It is her way of emphasising her
favourite theme: the relationship between prayer
and life, the balance between contemplation and
action. The only test that our journey has been
genuine is the fruit it bears in our Christian life:
action flows from contemplation, contemplation
nourishes life. Prayer and contemplation,
important as they are, unless they affect the way
we live will not serve to increase holiness. Growth
is the only sign of life: growth in love, growth in
service, growth in compassion – the compassion
of Christ.

Mary and Martha need each other; together
they express the fullness of Christian life: love in
service flowing from the hands of Martha and
the heart of Mary. Mary cannot be taken as an
exhaustive definition of contemplation, nor can
Martha be seen as fully expressing the demands of
ministry and service. They must both join together
in order to show hospitality and service to others.
The crucial test is the quality of our relationship

with Christ and our willingness to pour out our lives in the service of others. This is the reason for prayer, the purpose of every spiritual endeavour. Love cannot show its true depth apart from deeds of love.

Homecoming

In the journey towards the secret dwelling place of the soul, Teresa shows us how we can be transformed not only spiritually but humanly. Transformation into Christ does not imply any lessening of our humanity: self-transcendence means self-fulfilment at every level of our being. It is a journey towards wholeness: a kind of 'homecoming', a coming home to oneself. Human nature is not swallowed up by God: rather, it is enriched, being fully human, fully alive.

The person who is most truly and fully human is the one who has come closest to the source of all life, the place where light, truth and beauty dwell and radiate throughout the whole castle. The closer we come to our own centre, the closer we come to the ultimate centre of all things and to finding our place in the heart of the world. But the work of love is never done. We must not build castles in the air. 'The Lord doesn't look so much at the greatness of our works as at the love with which they are done.'[16]

It is with a sense of satisfaction and joy that Teresa looks back over the momentous journey she has traced. The labour was well spent, and she feels it will be a great consolation for her readers to take their delight in the castle of the soul. She even seems surprised and amazed at the wonders and riches she has discovered within! Although she spoke of no more than seven dwelling places, in each of these there are many others, with lovely gardens, fountains and labyrinths, things beautiful and bright to delight the soul and fill it with praise. A Garden of Eden.

Someday perhaps the inner light will shine forth from us, and then we'll need no other light
(Goethe)

And so, we have come full circle. The journey itself fades into the background. What matters now is 'how' we have travelled, and the longings and yearnings this has evoked. We have come to know that the land of heart's desire is within and discovered the pilgrim's way to it. The path is *prayer* – in which we gather up the fragments of our life and let ourselves be drawn into the radiant beauty of God and touch the transforming flow of divine energy. We discover who we really are, and what it means to be loved unconditionally.

The movement is away from self-absorption and predictable patterns towards an ever more complete participation in the life of the Trinity: the Father gazing at the Son, the Son gazing at the Father, and the gazing itself is the Holy Spirit. God is not a noun, he is a *verb*: he is life, energy and movement. So, too, is prayer. It can never be a concept or an idea: it is always life, friendship and love. Prayer is an act of the whole person responding to the divine call; we enter by the narrow gate and let go of whatever would hinder us along the way. It is a refusal to be side-tracked by fears, illusions or idle dreams. It is the very breath of the soul – a place of grace, freedom and homecoming.

As we look back with Teresa over the vast sweep of the journey she has travelled, we cannot but be encouraged by her enthusiasm and the clarity of her vision. She has shared not only a journey but a dream: *God's dream for us*. There is a call, an invitation: things can be different. The only limitation is that of our own fears. God's dream for us is greater than anything we can imagine for ourselves. We are the castle; it is real and it is within. We are called to grow, to explore the wonders hidden in our own heart. The Beloved is waiting to be our guide and companion. All we have to do is *want* to want him, to take the first step across the shaky drawbridge and follow the path through the darkness and into the light.

You know you will never get to the end
of the journey. But this, so far from discouraging,
only adds to the joy and glory of the climb.
On our journey, we cannot know what will
occur, just make the journey worth the taking
and pray that we are wiser
than we were at the beginning.[17]

Notes

1   Carolyn Humphreys, *From Ash to Fire: An Odyssey in Prayer – A Contemporary Journey through the Interior Castle of Teresa of Avila*, Hyde Park, NY: New City Press, 1992, p. 9.

2   *The Interior Castle* I:2:14, in *The Collected Works of St. Teresa of Avila*, vol. 2, Washington, DC: ICS Publications, 1980.

3   Cf. *ibid*. I:1:8; I:2:14. See the discussion 'The Lizards and the Snakes', in Julienne McLean, *Towards Mystical Union: A Modern Commentary on the Mystical Text The Interior Castle by St Teresa of Avila*, Second Edition, London: St Pauls, 2013, pp. 130-44.

4   *The Interior Castle* I:2:16.

5   *The Interior Castle* III:1:9.

6   From W B Yeats, 'Easter 1916'.

7   *The Interior Castle* IV:1:7.

8   *Spiritual Testimonies* 59:18, in *The Collected Works of St. Teresa of Avila*, vol. 1, Washington, DC: ICS Publications, 1987.

9   The title of a poem by Francis Thompson.

10 Adapted from T S Eliot, 'Little Gidding', line 254, in his *Four Quartets*.

11 *The Interior Castle* VI:10:7.

12 Cf. *Story of a Soul: The Autobiography of*

Saint Thérèse of Lisieux, Washington, DC: ICS Publications, 1996, p. 193. The quotation on the next line, 'infinite horizons', is from her Letter 226, in *Saint Thérèse of Lisieux: General Correspondence*, vol. 2, Washington, DC: ICS Publications, 1988.

13 From Patrick Kavanagh, 'The Great Hunger', part VI.

14 *The Ascent of Mount Carmel*, Book 2, 16:8, in *The Collected Works of Saint John of the Cross*, Washington, DC: ICS Publications, 1991.

15 *The Interior Castle* VII:2:11 (from the translation by E Allison Peers, in *The Complete Works of Saint Teresa of Jesus*, vol. II, London: Sheed & Ward, 1946).

16 *The Interior Castle* VII:4:15 (translation of ICS Publications).

17 By Winston Churchill.

TERESIAN PRESS
PUBLICATIONS AVAILABLE

St Teresa and the Our Father: A Catechism of Prayer
Aloysius Rego, OCD
£6.00

Praying with St Teresa through The Way of Perfection
Jerome Lantry, OCD
£5.00

The Writings of St Teresa of Avila: An Introduction
Eugene McCaffrey, OCD
£5.00

John of the Cross: Seasons of Prayer
Iain Matthew, OCD
£5.00

Infinite Horizons: Scripture through Carmelite Eyes
James McCaffrey, OCD
£8.00

Elizabeth of the Trinity: The Unfolding of her Message
Joanne Mosley
2 volumes, £10.00 each volume

Holiness For All: Themes from St Thérèse of Lisieux
Aloysius Rego, OCD
£7.00

Upon This Mountain: Prayer in the Carmelite Tradition
Mary McCormack, OCD
£4.00

Let Yourself Be Loved: Elizabeth of the Trinity
Eugene McCaffrey, OCD
£5.00

TERESIAN PRESS
SOME FORTHCOMING PUBLICATIONS

Living with God: St Teresa's Understanding of Prayer
Tomás Álvarez, OCD

A Moment of Prayer – A Life of Prayer
Conrad De Meester, OCD

St Paul: A Gospel of Prayer
James McCaffrey, OCD

What Carmel Means to Me
Edited by James McCaffrey, OCD & Joanne Mosley

*Captive Flames: A Biblical Reading of
the Carmelite Saints – **to be reissued***
James McCaffrey, OCD

Teresian Press
Carmelite Priory
Boars Hill
Oxford OX1 5HB

www.carmelitebooks.com

MOUNT CARMEL

A REVIEW OF THE SPIRITUAL LIFE

The flagship magazine of the Teresian Carmelites
of Great Britain and Ireland